European Computer Driving Licence®

Syllabus 5.0

Module 7 - Web Browsing & Communication

7b Communication using Outlook 2007

Release ECDL259v1

Published by:

CiA Training Ltd
Business & Innovation Centre
Sunderland Enterprise Park
Sunderland SR5 2TH
United Kingdom

Tel: +44 (0) 191 549 5002
Fax: +44 (0) 191 549 9005

E-mail: info@ciatraining.co.uk
Web: www.ciatraining.co.uk

ISBN-13: 978 1 86005 685 7

Acknowledgements:

The European Computer Driving Licence is operated in Ireland by ICS
Skills, the training and certification body of the Irish Computer Society.
Candidates using this courseware should register online with ICS Skills
through an approved ECDL Test Centre. Without a valid registration, and
the allocation of a unique ICS Skills ID number or SkillsCard, no ECDL
tests can be taken and no certificate, or any other form of recognition, can
be given to a candidate.

Other ECDL Foundation Certification programmes offered by ICS Skills
include Equalskills, ECDL Advanced, ECDL WebStarter, ECDL
ImageMaker, EUCIP and Certified Training Professional.

Contact: ICS Skills
             Crescent Hall
             Mount Street Crescent
             Dublin 2
             Ireland

Website: www.ics.ie/skills
Email: *skills@ics.ie*

First published 2008

European Computer Driving Licence, ECDL, International Computer Driving Licence, ICDL, e-Citizen and related logos are all registered Trade Marks of The European Computer Driving Licence Foundation Limited ("ECDL Foundation").

CiA Training Ltd is an entity independent of ECDL Foundation and is not associated with ECDL Foundation in any manner. This courseware may be used to assist candidates to prepare for the ECDL Foundation Certification Programme as titled on the courseware. Neither ECDL Foundation nor **CiA Training Ltd** warrants that the use of this courseware publication will ensure passing of the tests for that ECDL Foundation Certification Programme. This courseware publication has been independently reviewed and approved by ECDL Foundation as covering the learning objectives for the ECDL Foundation Certification Programme.

Confirmation of this approval can be obtained by reviewing the Partners Page in the About Us Section of the website www.ecdl.org

The material contained in this courseware publication has not been reviewed for technical accuracy and does not guarantee that candidates will pass the test for the ECDL Foundation Certification Programme. Any and all assessment items and/or performance-based exercises contained in this courseware relate solely to this publication and do not constitute or imply certification by ECDL Foundation in respect of the ECDL Foundation Certification Programme or any other ECDL Foundation test. Irrespective of how the material contained in this courseware is deployed, for example in a learning management system (LMS) or a customised interface, nothing should suggest to the candidate that this material constitutes certification or can lead to certification through any other process than official ECDL Foundation certification testing.

For details on sitting a test for an ECDL Foundation certification programme, please contact your country's designated National Licensee or visit the ECDL Foundation's website at www.ecdl.org.

Candidates using this courseware must be registered with the National Operator before undertaking a test for an ECDL Foundation Certification Programme. Without a valid registration, the test(s) cannot be undertaken and no certificate, nor any other form of recognition, can be given to a candidate.

Registration should be undertaken with your country's designated National Licensee at an Approved Test Centre.

Downloading the Data Files

The data associated with these exercises must be downloaded from our website. Go to: *www.ciatraining.co.uk/data*. Follow the on screen instructions to download the appropriate data files.

By default, the data files will be downloaded to **Documents \ CIA DATA FILES \ ECDL**. Users of *Windows XP*, replace **Documents** with **My Documents**.

If you prefer, the data can be supplied on CD at an additional cost. Contact the Sales team at *info@ciatraining.co.uk*.

Aims

To demonstrate the ability to use an e-mail application on a personal computer. To create and send e-mail and to manage personal Contact Groups and message folders.

Objectives

After completing the guide the user will be able to:

- Understand what e-mail is and know some advantages and disadvantages of its use. Be aware of other communication options; be aware of network etiquette and security considerations when using e-mail

- Create, spell check and send e-mail. Reply to and forward e-mail, handle file attachments and print an e-mail

- Be aware of ways to enhance productivity when working with e-mail software. Organise and manage e-mail

Assessment of Knowledge

At the end of this guide is a section called the **Record of Achievement Matrix**. Before the guide is started it is recommended that the user complete the matrix to measure the level of current knowledge.

Tick boxes are provided for each feature. **1** is for no knowledge, **2** some knowledge and **3** is for competent.

After working through a section, complete the **Record of Achievement** matrix for that section and only when competent in all areas move on to the next section.

Contents

SECTION 1 OUTLOOK 7

1 - USING E-MAIL 8

2 - USING OUTLOOK 10

3 - E-MAIL HELP 12

4 - CHANGING SCREEN DISPLAY 13

5 - MESSAGE HEADINGS 15

6 - CLOSING OUTLOOK 17

7 - REVISION 18

SECTION 2 MESSAGE EDITING 19

8 - CREATING A MESSAGE 20

9 - CUT, COPY AND PASTE MESSAGES 22

10 - CUT, COPY AND PASTE FROM WORD 23

11 - SPELL CHECKER 24

12 - APPLYING A SIGNATURE 26

13 - REVISION 28

14 - REVISION 29

SECTION 3 SEND AND RECEIVE 30

15 - SENDING MESSAGES 31

16 - OPEN AND READ MESSAGES 32

17 - FLAGGING A MESSAGE 33

18 - ATTACHING FILES 34

19 - OPEN AND SAVE A FILE ATTACHMENT 35

20 - CHANGING MESSAGE PRIORITY 37

21 - REPLY TO/FORWARD MESSAGES 38

22 - CONTACTS 40

23 - ADD SENDER TO CONTACTS 41

24 - DISTRIBUTION LISTS 42

25 - REVISION 44

26 - REVISION 45

27 - REVISION 46

SECTION 4 MESSAGE MANAGEMENT 47

    28 - SAVE A DRAFT MESSAGE 48

    29 - PRINTING A MESSAGE 49

    30 - DELETING MESSAGES 50

    31 - CREATING INBOX FOLDERS 51

    32 - ORGANISING MESSAGES 53

    33 - FINDING MESSAGES 54

    34 - REVISION 56

ANSWERS...57

GLOSSARY 58

INDEX 59

RECORD OF ACHIEVEMENT MATRIX 61

OTHER PRODUCTS FROM CIA TRAINING 63

Section 1
Outlook

By the end of this Section you should be able to:

Understand Electronic Messaging and Related Issues

Use Online Help

Use e-mail

Change Screen Display

Close Outlook

To gain an understanding of the above features, work through the **Driving Lessons** in this **Section**.

For each **Driving Lesson**, read the **Park and Read** instructions, without touching the keyboard, then work through the numbered steps of the **Manoeuvres** on the computer. Complete the **Revision Exercise(s)** at the end of the section to test your knowledge.

Driving Lesson 1 - Using E-mail

▣ Park and Read

Today e-mail is an extremely important business tool and many businesses would almost come to a standstill without it. It has obvious advantages over the normal postal system: it is much faster - mail is delivered within seconds. Rather than pay excessive postage for sending paper copies of files through the post or by courier, electronic files can be attached to e-mail messages. All the sender pays is the cost of a local telephone call, or probably a lot less if they have a broadband connection. Consider how much more quickly business documents can be sent overseas using e-mail than by using surface or airmail. A point of note is that some anti-virus software/firewalls prevent certain types of attachment, which contain macros (such as databases) passing through. This is because some viruses use macros to work.

As it is possible to set up an e-mail account that is **web based**, rather than an account linked to a specific computer, messages can be collected and sent from any computer with an Internet connection, anywhere in the world. After having set up your account, it's a simple matter of logging on to send or read your messages. One disadvantage of web based accounts is that disk space is limited. This means that you need to keep an eye on the size of messages in your inbox; it can also prevent messages with large attachments getting through.

Before using e-mail, familiarise yourself with the rules of **netiquette** - network etiquette. Always use accurate and brief subjects in the appropriate field on a message. Keep your messages brief and relevant rather than rambling. Ask before sending large attachments; don't send heated messages (**flames**); don't use all UPPERCASE – it is the same as shouting; when replying, always make sure the subject is still relevant to your reply. Consider the implications very carefully before sending any sensitive information by e-mail. In a work situation, you must familiarise yourself with the e-mail policy in place. Usually, common business rules and regulations state that you must not send messages that might offend, or jokes, etc. Never send "chain letters". Basically only subject matter directly associated with the business should be sent via e-mail.

Make sure your outgoing messages are spelled correctly, just as you would before sending a letter. Many e-mail programs allow you to format messages with different colours, fonts and backgrounds. This provides an opportunity to show some individuality.

Unwanted Messages
Be prepared to receive unwanted e-mails. Certain companies and individuals send out masses of junk mail. You are shown later in the guide how to delete messages, so this should be useful. However, many of these types of messages have a link near the bottom that allows you to **unsubscribe**, so no further messages will be sent to you. It is always worth scanning the message for something like this.

Driving Lesson 1 - Continued

As was mentioned earlier in the Internet section, be vigilant about e-mail messages; they can contain viruses. Ensure you have up to date anti-virus software installed on your computer. Messages without a subject or from an unknown source should be treated with caution. <u>Save attached files to disk and scan them before opening if you are at all suspicious</u>. If you do open a message attachment that contains a virus, the results can be disastrous for your computer.

To send messages securely (encrypted), you can set them up to be signed digitally. A personal certificate is obtained by the individual to verify his identity and optionally encrypt transmissions. This is called a **digital signature**.

Any message, whether received via e-mail or through the door, which promises riches, prizes, or rewards in return for a cash payment or supplying your bank/credit card details should be regarded with the suspicion it deserves and be deleted or thrown away immediately. Some more subtle tricks have included official-looking e-mails supposedly from banks, etc., asking you to confirm card details and/or PIN numbers. This is known as **phishing**. Delete them. Banks will <u>never</u> ask for such information to be put in an e-mail. Be very careful who you give personal information to – **identity theft** is also a risk with e-mail. Take as much care to protect your privacy while using e-mail as you would in shredding normal mail before putting it in the bin.

On a slightly less serious level, false messages have appeared warning you that you have a virus on your computer and you must delete certain files to remove it. When you do this you find that your computer will no longer function.

Be suspicious of all e-mails from unknown sources. If in doubt, it is a good idea to get a second opinion. Preferably ask someone with experience of Internet and e-mail matters and whose opinion you trust.

Driving Lesson 2 - Using Outlook

▣ Park and Read

For many people who are connected to the Internet, the majority of their online time is often spent sending or receiving e-mail messages and there are many applications which will control this function on your computer.

Microsoft Outlook 2007 is one such application that manages all electronic messages, both e-mail and newsgroup mail, coming to and going from the computer. Messages can easily be composed and sent to any e-mail address; files can be attached to a message in a couple of steps. *Microsoft Outlook 2007* is supplied as part of *Microsoft Office 2007*.

If a user is not using *Microsoft Outlook*, messages are stored for them until they are collected.

A very useful feature of the program is the **Contacts**, which stores information about contacts. If a contact's e-mail address is entered here, it saves the need for remembering addresses.

If a user wishes to subscribe to **Newsgroups**, *Outlook* can be configured to receive any newsgroup post. Newsgroup messages are sent in the same way as e-mail messages.

E-mail addresses

E-mail addresses are needed before a user can send or receive mail. An address consists of:

a **user name** -	the name of the mailbox where the server forwards incoming mail.
an **@ sign** -	separates the user name from the domain name.
a **host name** -	the address of the computer which sends and receives mail.

↱ Manoeuvres

1.   To start *Outlook*, select **Start | All Programs | Microsoft Office | Microsoft Office Outlook 2007**. Alternatively there may be icons to start Outlook on the **Start Menu** itself, , on the **Desktop**, or on the **Quick Launch** section of the **Taskbar**.

ℹ️ *Outlook must be configured before it can be used for the first time. Configuring is simply the term used to describe the supply of user information to the server, who "manages" the mail. Once the required information has been supplied, e-mail can be used. If the **Internet Connection Wizard** starts, contact your IT Administrator, who will be able to configure a personal **Outlook** profile for you.*

Driving Lesson 2 - Continued

2. Assuming that an Internet connection is active the *Outlook* window will be displayed. The first time *Outlook* is opened, the Outlook Today screen will be shown. Many users subsequently change their settings so that the e-mail **Inbox** is the first screen shown.

i *If you are accessing the Internet via a server you may first be asked to logon to the network, or if there is more than one e-mail account available on the computer you may have to select one.*

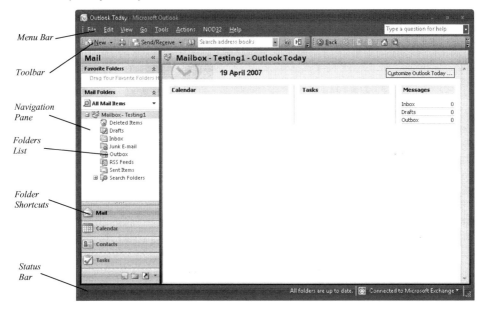

i *The screen may not look exactly like this as there are many display options available (see Driving Lesson 4). This picture shows the **Navigation Pane** displayed, the **Mail** shortcut selected and the **Outlook Today** screen shown.*

3. Click **Customize Outlook Today** on the **Folder Banner**.

4. There is an option **When starting, go directly to Outlook Today**. If this is unchecked, the **Inbox** will be the first folder shown on starting *Outlook*. Set this option to your own preference and click **Save Changes**.

5. If the **Inbox** is not displayed in the main part of the window, select it now by clicking **Inbox** from the **Folders List** in the **Navigation Pane**.

6. Leave the *Outlook* window open for the next Driving Lesson.

Driving Lesson 3 - E-mail Help

P Park and Read

Outlook contains an online **Help** facility that may assist when certain problems are experienced.

Manoeuvres

1. Select **Help | Microsoft Office Outlook Help** or click the 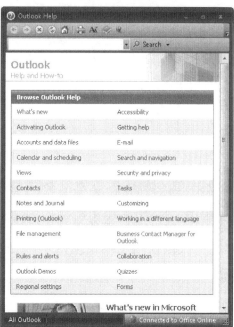 button on the **Toolbar**. The **Outlook Help** window is displayed, showing a list of help topics.

2. Click on **Views**. Further topics are listed. Click on a topic to display help text, then use the **Back** button, , to return to the main help display.

3. An alternative method of searching for help is to use the **Table of Contents**. Click the **Show Table of Contents** button, .

4. The **Table of Contents** panel is displayed on the left. Click **Views** this displays a list of topics from which to choose.

5. Click **Preview messages**. The help text is displayed on the right.

6. The **Table of Contents** panel can be hidden, click the **Hide Table of Contents** button, .

7. Type **signature** in the search box at the top and click .

8. Click on one of the result topics and read the text.

9. Close the **Help** window, but leave *Outlook* open.

i *Clicking **Microsoft Office Online** from the **Help** menu will open an Online help web page with links to a variety of topics.*

Driving Lesson 4 - Changing Screen Display

Park and Read

Outlook has a **Folders List** at the left of the screen, which contains a list of the various folders available, e.g. **Inbox**, **Sent Items**, etc. The display changes depending on the folder selected. It is also possible to change the main screen **View**, e.g. whether to preview messages before opening or not, or whether to display the list of folders permanently.

Manoeuvres

1.   If the **Inbox** is not displayed in the main part of the window, select it now by clicking **Inbox** from the **Folders List** in the **Navigation Pane**.

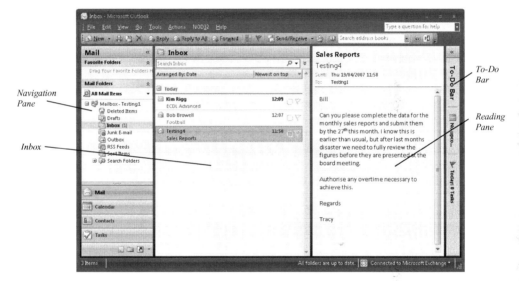

*The layout of this screen is optional. The example above shows the **Navigation Pane**, the **Reading Pane** on the right and the **To-Do Bar** minimised.*

2.   Look at the **Inbox** which lists messages received. Messages in **bold** type have not been read yet. Those messages which are <u>not</u> bold have been read. Notice the different icons to the left of the messages.

3.   To see only messages which have not been read, select **View | Current View** and check **Unread Messages in This Folder**.

4.   To see all messages again, select **View | Current View** and check **Messages**.

Driving Lesson 4 - Continued

5. Select any message in the **Inbox** and its contents are previewed in the **Reading Pane**.

6. The **Reading Pane** can be hidden. Select **View | Reading Pane** and click the **Off** option.

7. Select **View | Reading Pane** and click the **Bottom** option to show the **Reading Pane** underneath the **Inbox** list.

> *The sizes of the **Inbox** list and the **Reading Pane** can be adjusted by clicking and dragging the boundary line between them.*

8. To remove the **To-Do Bar**, select **View | To-Do Bar** and click **Off**.

9. Select **View | Toolbars** to list the available toolbars for this window. Any toolbar with a tick next to it is currently displayed. Click **Advanced** to select that toolbar. The window should now look like this.

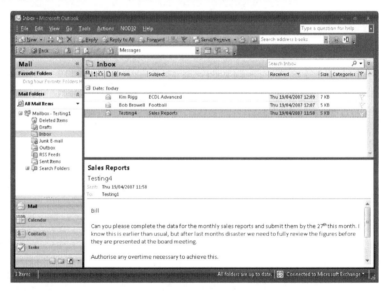

10. Only the **Standard** toolbar is required for this guide, select **View | Toolbars** and remove the check from **Advanced**.

11. Select **View | Toolbars** and click **Customize**. There are options here to change which buttons appear on the toolbar and to change their appearance. Look at the options, then click the **Close** button to return to the **Inbox**.

12. Select **View | Current View | Messages** to make sure that all messages, read and unread, are shown in the **Inbox**.

Driving Lesson 5 - Message Headings

P Park and Read

The display of message headings in the **Inbox** can be changed to suit the user.

Manoeuvres

1. The messages listed in the **Inbox** have information displayed in columns.

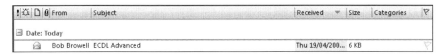

2. The way in which this information is displayed can be varied. To remove the date grouping select **View | Arrange By** and select **Show in Groups** to deselect it.

3. Select **View | Current View | Customize Current View**. Note there are options here to format, group, sort and filter the **Inbox** messages. This can be useful when there are a large number of messages in the **Inbox**.

4. Click the **Fields** button. The **Show Fields** dialog box is displayed.

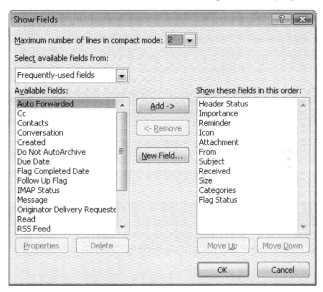

5. The list on the right shows all the fields currently displayed. Compare it with the first picture in this driving lesson. The left side of the dialog box shows all the available fields that can be used in the list.

Driving Lesson 5 - Continued

6.   Click on **Categories** from the list on the right then click the **Remove** button. The field is removed from the list.

7.   Click on **Cc** from the list on the left then click the **Add** button. The field is added to the bottom of the list on the right.

8.   With the **Cc** field still selected, click the **Move Up** button until the field is positioned between **Subject** and **Received** (this is the date an e-mail is received).

9.   Click **OK**, then **OK** at the **Customize View** dialog box. The new column headings are shown in the **Inbox**.

The width of individual columns can be varied by clicking and dragging the column boundaries on the header row.

10.   To replace the headings in their original location and restore the grouping by date, select **View | Current View | Customize Current View**, then click the **Reset Current View** button.

11.   Click **OK** and then **OK** again to perform the action.

*The **Flag Status** field always appears as the last field on the right.*

Driving Lesson 6 - Closing Outlook

▣ Park and Read

Outlook can be closed at any time. With a dial up connection make sure the Internet connection is also terminated, if no prompt to disconnect appears.

Whilst *Outlook* is disconnected, incoming messages will continue to be received and held, either by your mail service provider or your server. When you next connect, all waiting messages will be passed to your **Inbox**.

⌐ Manoeuvres

1.   Click the **Close** button on the **Menu Bar** at the top right of the screen.

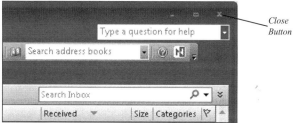

Close Button

ℹ️ *Alternatively, select **File | Exit** from the menus.*

2.   If you have a dial up connection the **Auto Disconnect** dialog box should appear. Select **Disconnect Now** if you wish to end the current session.

3.   For dial up connections <u>only</u>, if the **Auto Disconnect** dialog box is not displayed, double click the **Connection** icon, ▨, in the **Taskbar** and click **Disconnect**.

Driving Lesson 7 - Revision

This covers the features introduced in this section. Try not to refer to the preceding Driving Lessons while completing it.

1. List some advantages of using e-mail in a business environment.

2. What is netiquette?

3. What can gain access to your computer via e-mail messages?

4. What can you do to protect your computer?

5. What is e-mail?

6. What are the three sections of an e-mail address?

7. Start *Outlook*.

8. Hide all **Toolbars** and the **Reading Pane**.

9. Replace the screen elements in their original positions.

10. View the **Show Fields** dialog box which allows the **Inbox** fields to be changed.

11. View only the following fields in the order stated: **Attachment**, **Flag**, **Priority**, **From**, **Received**, **Subject**.

12. Reset the message headings to their original values.

13. Close *Outlook*.

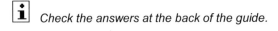 *Check the answers at the back of the guide.*

If you experienced any difficulty completing the Revision, refer back to the Driving Lessons in this section. Then redo the Revision.

Once you are confident with the features, complete the Record of Achievement Matrix referring to the section at the end of the guide. Only when competent move on to the next Section.

Section 2
Message Editing

By the end of this Section you should be able to:

Create a Message

Insert and Delete Text

Cut, Copy and Paste Messages

Cut and Paste from Word

Use the Spell Checker

Add an AutoSignature to a Message

To gain an understanding of the above features, work through the **Driving Lessons** in this **Section**.

For each **Driving Lesson**, read the **Park and Read** instructions, without touching the keyboard, then work through the numbered steps of the **Manoeuvres** on the computer. Complete the **Revision Exercise(s)** at the end of the section to test your knowledge.

Driving Lesson 8 - Creating a Message

▣ Park and Read

Outlook allows the user to send an e-mail message to anyone on the Internet, as long as his or her address is known.

☞ Manoeuvres

1. Start *Outlook* and select the **File | New** to show a list of all the objects that can be created in *Outlook*. Most of these are outside the scope of this guide.

2. Select **Mail Message** from the top of the list. The **Untitled Message** window is displayed with the **Message** tab selected in the **Ribbon** area.

ℹ *The **New Mail Message** button,* *, can also be used to display the **New Message** window.*

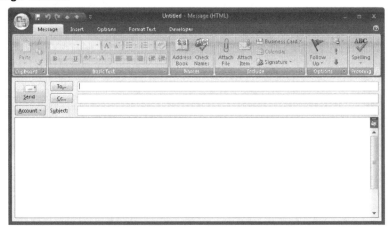

3. The **Ribbon** can be minimized to display more space for the message. Right click on the **Ribbon** and select **Minimize the Ribbon**.

4. The **Ribbon** tabs are still displayed, click **Message** and the **Message** tab is temporarily displayed. Click away from the **Ribbon** and it is minimized again.

5. Type your own e-mail address in the **To** box.

6. You may also have addresses listed in an **Address Book** (see Driving Lesson 22). Click the **To** button, ⎡ To... ⎤. Double click on any name from the list and click **OK**. The message is now addressed to two people.

☞

Driving Lesson 8 - Continued

7. In the **Subject** box, enter **Sending messages**.

8. Type in the following text in the main part of the window:
   Always remember to check your e-mail regularly!

9. Double click on the word **regularly** to select it, then press **<Delete>**. Insert the new text **at regular intervals throughout the day!**

i *Methods for inserting, deleting and formatting text in Outlook are the same as in most word processing packages.*

10. Press **<Enter>** to start a new line and type **You don't want to miss important messages**.

11. Before adding formatting to the text the **Ribbon** can be restored, so that it is visible all the time. Right click on any **Ribbon** tab and select **Minimize the Ribbon** to remove the check and display the **Ribbon** in full.

12. Select the two sentences. You are going to change their formatting. Make sure both sentences remain selected as each of the following effects are applied.

13. Look at the **Basic Text** group of buttons on the **Message** tab. Click on the **Font** drop down arrow, Calibri (Bo ▾ and select **Comic Sans MS**.

14. With the text still highlighted, use the **Font Size** button, 11 ▾ , to change the text to **12pt** and embolden the text by clicking the **Bold** button, **B** .

15. Change the text to bulleted points by clicking **Bullets**, ▤▾

16. Indent the bulleted list to the right by clicking **Increase Indent**, ▤ .

17. Click **Decrease Indent**, ▤ , to replace the bullets in their original position.

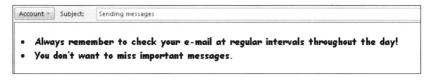

18. Use the alignment buttons, ☰ ☰ ☰ , to see the effect of changing the layout of the text.

19. Finally make sure the text is left aligned.

20. Leave the message open for the next Driving Lesson.

Driving Lesson 9 - Cut, Copy and Paste Messages

Park and Read

It is possible to cut, copy and paste text to a different location within a message or to a different message entirely.

Manoeuvres

1. Using the e-mail created in the previous Driving Lesson, use click and drag to select all the sentences.

2. From the **Message** tab, click  or press **<Ctrl C>**. The original text is left in the message, but a copy of it is now written to a temporary area of storage called the **Clipboard**.

3. Position the cursor at the end of the text, then press **<Enter>** to create a new line.

4. Click the **Paste** button from the **Message** tab or press **<Ctrl V>** to paste the copied text from the **Clipboard** into the message at the point where the cursor is flashing.

*Cut or copied text remains on the **Clipboard** until another item is cut or copied. It can be pasted as many times as desired.*

5. Now select the first sentence and click **Cut** or press **<Ctrl X>**. The text is removed from the message to the **Clipboard**.

6. Position the cursor at the end of the text and **Paste** in the cut text.

7. Minimise the message window to display the main *Outlook* window. Click **New Mail Message**, **New** and enter **Pasting** in the **Subject** box. The title bar of the message now shows **Pasting**.

8. With the cursor in the message area, paste the text. The text from the first message (**Sending Messages**) is pasted into the new message.

9. Click the **Sending Messages** button on the **Taskbar** to redisplay the window.

10. At the end of the message type **Regards** and your name. Copy this new text and use the **Taskbar** to return to the **Pasting** message.

11. Paste in the copied text at the end of the **Pasting** message.

12. Close the **Pasting** message by clicking the **Close** button, **X**, at the right of its **Title Bar**. Select **No** if a prompt to save appears.

13. Close the **Sending Messages** message window without saving.

Driving Lesson 10 - Cut, Copy and Paste from Word

▣ Park and Read

It is possible to cut or copy text from a *Word* document and paste it into an e-mail message, so that time is not spent re-entering the same text. If the entire document was to be used in the message, it is more usual to attach the file. This will be discussed in **Section 3**.

↱ Manoeuvres

1.   Close *Outlook*, then start *Word* (**Start | All Programs | Microsoft Word**).

2.   Type in the following text:

     To save myself time and money, I can use existing text in my Outlook messages.

3.   Select the text and select to copy in *Word* to copy the text.

4.   Click the **Office** button, , and select to close *Word*. Do not save any changes.

5.   Open *Outlook* and start a new message.

6.   Click within the message box to place the cursor and either click the **Paste** button or press <**Ctrl V**> to paste in the text created in *Word*.

7.   If necessary, insert a space at the end of the text and type:

     This text has been pasted in from a word processing application.

8.   Click and drag to select **a word processing application**.

9.   This text is to be deleted. Press <**Delete**> to remove it.

10. Replace the deleted text with **Microsoft Word**.

11. Close the message without saving.

Driving Lesson 11 - Spell Checker

▣ Park and Read

Outlook contains a spell-checking feature, which can be used to check spelling of all messages before they are sent. The spell checker is very similar to the one available in *Word*.

If none of the required applications are present this lesson can only be read for information.

↱ Manoeuvres

1. Create a new message with intentional spelling mistakes like the one in the diagram below.

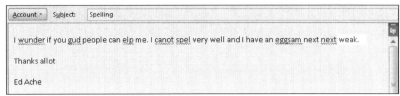

ⓘ *The option to underline spelling mistakes in red as you enter the text (as seen in the picture), is described later in this lesson.*

2. Click the **Spelling** button, ![ABC Spelling], to check the message for errors. The **Spelling and Grammar** dialog box appears highlighting the first word that the spell checker does not recognise (wunder).

Driving Lesson 11 - Continued

3. There are options to leave the word as it is (**Ignore**) or **Change** it. Select the correct choice from the **Suggestions** list (wonder) and click **Change**.

4. The word is changed in the message and the spell checker moves on to the next unknown word.

5. Click **Change** to replace the word. Process the remaining errors as they are found, either changing or ignoring them.

6. The spell checker will find duplicated words, not spelling errors as such - click the **Delete** button in the dialog box to remove one of the duplications.

7. Click **OK** when the message appears to say the check is complete.

8. The spell checker only highlights words that are not in its dictionary, **weak** and **allot** are both incorrect in this message but because they are valid words they will not be highlighted. Correct the words manually.

9. Close the message without saving.

10. From the main *Outlook* window, select **Tools | Options**

11. Display the **Spelling** tab in the dialog box. There is an option here to **Always check spelling before sending**. Tick this option if you want all messages to be spell checked automatically before being sent out.

12. Click the **Spelling and AutoCorrection** button in the dialog box. Examine all the options which control how the spell checker works.

13. There is an option to **Check spelling as you type**. Tick this option if you want spelling mistakes to be highlighted (with red underline) as you are entering text.

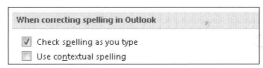

14. Click **OK** to close the **Editor Options** dialog box, then **OK** to close the main **Options** dialog box.

Driving Lesson 12 - Applying a Signature

▣ Park and Read

A personal signature can be added to the end of each e-mail message automatically, without the need for typing it each time. Several signatures can exist within *Outlook* and the appropriate one can be selected for any message.

☞ Manoeuvres

1. To create a signature, select **Tools | Options** and the **Mail Format** tab.

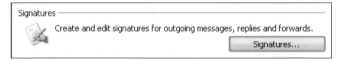

2. Click **Signatures**.

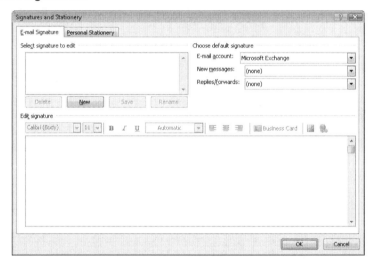

3. Click the **New** button. Enter a name for your signature, e.g. **Full Title** where prompted and click **OK**.

4. In the large **Edit signature** box, enter your name as the signature text, and, on the next lines, a job title, e.g.

        Kate Jones
        Financial Controller
        Midlands Division

Driving Lesson 12 - Continued

5.   Highlight your name and click the drop down arrow on the **Font** button,

     | Calibri (Body) ▼ |
     .

6.   Scroll down the list of fonts and select **Freestyle Script** (or similar) and a
     Size of **24** point.

Several signatures can be added in this way to cover various situations.

7.   To add this signature automatically to all new messages, click the drop
     down arrow in the **New Messages** box and select **Full Title**.

8.   Click **OK** and **OK** again at the options dialog box.

9.   Start a new message. Enter any address in the **To** box and enter
     Signature as the **Subject**. The signature automatically appears in the
     message area. Highlight the signature text and delete it.

10. To add a signature manually, display the **Insert** tab in the **Ribbon** and
     click the **Signature** button. A list of all available signatures will be shown.
     Select **Full Title** and it will appear in the message.

11. Close the message without saving.

12. To stop the signature appearing automatically, select **Tools | Options**
     and the **Mail Format** tab then click **Signatures**.

13. Drop down the list for **New messages** and select **<none>**.

14. To delete a signature altogether, select it from the list on the left of the
     dialog box and click **Delete**. Select **Yes** at the confirmation.

15. Click **OK** and **OK** again at the options dialog box.

Driving Lesson 13 - Revision

This covers the features introduced in this section. Try not to refer to the preceding Driving Lessons while completing it.

1. Compose a new message and address it to a friend.

2. Enter the subject as **Holiday**.

3. Enter the following message:

    Dear…

    I've just heard that you're going on holiday to Egypt and will be visiting the Valley of the Kings. Here's something that may interest you.

    Enjoy your holiday.

4. Press <**Enter**> and open *Word*. Open the **Kingtut** file from the **3 Word Processing** data files folder.

5. Copy the first four paragraphs, then close *Word* <u>without</u> saving.

6. Paste the text into the e-mail message.

7. Delete the text **the "boy king", as he is often called,**.

8. Cut **Enjoy your holiday.** from the original message text and paste it at the end of the message after the imported text.

9. Spell check the message.

10. Close the message <u>without</u> saving.

If you experienced any difficulty completing the Revision, refer back to the Driving Lessons in this section. Then redo the Revision.

Driving Lesson 14 - Revision

This covers the features introduced in this section. Try not to refer to the preceding Driving Lessons while completing it.

1.   Start a new message.

2.   Address it to a friend.

3.   The subject is **Viruses**.

4.   Enter this message:

      I thought I should warn you that e-mail messages can contain viruses. Make sure your anti-virus software is up to date.

5.   Create an informal signature for yourself.

6.   Add it to the message.

7.   Close the message <u>without</u> saving.

8.   Delete your signature from the **Options** dialog box.

If you experienced any difficulty completing the Revision, refer back to the Driving Lessons in this section. Then redo the Revision.

Once you are confident with the features, complete the Record of Achievement Matrix referring to the section at the end of the guide. Only when competent move on to the next Section.

Section 3
Send and Receive

By the end of this Section you should be able to:

Send, Open, Read and Flag Messages

Attach Files

Change Message Priority

Reply to and Forward Messages

Use Contacts

Add Sender to Contacts

Create and Use a Distribution List

To gain an understanding of the above features, work through the **Driving Lessons** in this **Section**.

For each **Driving Lesson**, read the **Park and Read** instructions, without touching the keyboard, then work through the numbered steps of the **Manoeuvres** on the computer. Complete the **Revision Exercise(s)** at the end of the section to test your knowledge.

Driving Lesson 15 - Sending Messages

🅿 Park and Read

Outlook allows the user to send an e-mail message to anyone on the Internet, as long as his or her address is known.

Manoeuvres

1.   Click **New ▾** to start a new message.

2.   Enter your own e-mail address in the **To** box, so the message will come back to you and the results of this Driving Lesson can be observed.

3.   In the **Subject** box, enter **Test message**.

4.   A carbon copy of this message can be sent to another recipient who needs to take some action on it. Click in the **Cc** box and type in the e-mail address of a friend.

5.   **Bcc** stands for **blind carbon copy**. To make this box available, display the **Options** tab and click **Show Bcc** from the **Fields** group. Use the **Bcc** box to send a copy of a message to someone who needs to know about the original message, but is not required to take any action on it. Other addressees are not aware if a blind carbon copy is sent. Enter a friend's e-mail address in the **Bcc** field (a different to the one in the previous step).

6.   Type in the following message text:

     E-mail can be used to catch up with your friends, wherever they are, for the cost of a local telephone call.

7.   Click **Send** to send the message to the **Outbox** ready to be sent. The message may be sent from here immediately.

8.   If the **Outbox** still shows the message, send it to the server (where it is then forwarded to its destination), by clicking **Send/Receive**. When this button is clicked, *Outlook* also checks for any incoming mail.

9.   When the message has been sent, click on the **Sent Items** folder in the **Navigation Pane**. A copy of all sent messages is kept here (optionally).

ℹ️ *The options to send messages immediately and save copies in the **Sent Items** folders can be set or cleared using **Tools | Options**, **Preferences** tab, **E-mail Options**.*

10. It can sometimes take a few minutes for messages to be received. Check with your friends that they received the message.

Driving Lesson 16 - Open and Read Messages

▣ Park and Read

Messages are received in the **Inbox** and are shown in bold type, with an unopened envelope icon next to the sender's information, ✉ **Gillian Atkinson**. Once a message has been read, its icon changes to an opened envelope, ✉.

⌒ Manoeuvres

1. Click the **Send/Receive** button, 📥 Send/Receive and a dialog box will briefly appear to say *Outlook* is checking for new messages.

2. Display the **Inbox** and watch the new messages appear in the message pane. There should be at least one message (**Test message**, sent to yourself earlier).

i *If the message has not arrived, wait for a few minutes and try Send and Receive again.*

3. To read a message, either click on it once, then view its contents in the **Reading Pane**, or double click to see the whole message, including the sender's e-mail address. Click on the **Test message** and read its contents in the **Reading Pane**.

4. By default, the message will be marked as read as soon as another message is selected or the display is changed, but this can be changed. Select **Tools | Options** and click the **Other** tab.

5. Click the **Reading Pane** button.

6. The default setting is shown. Selecting **Mark items as read when viewed in the Reading Pane** and setting a **Wait** time will change the way messages are marked as read. Unchecking both of the first two options will mean

that messages are never marked as read by appearing in the **Reading Pane**. Click **Cancel** to leave the setting unchanged. Click **Cancel** again.

7. To mark the **Test message** as **Unread**, select it, then select **Edit | Mark as Unread**. The envelope icon changes to closed and the text to bold type.

8. Read any other messages which are present.

9. Double click on the **Test message** to open it.

10. Close the message window by clicking the **Close** button, ✖.

Driving Lesson 17 - Flagging a Message

Park and Read

A message can be **flagged** to indicate that further actions need to be carried out on the message, such as a follow up call, reply, etc. The flag action can have a start date, a due date and a completed date. You can also add a complete by date to the flag action, which will display a reminder.

Manoeuvres

1. Select a message in the **Inbox** and click **Follow Up**, 🏳 on the toolbar.

> *The same **Follow Up** button is also available from the **Ribbon** when a message is opened.*

2. Click **Custom** from the **Follow Up** options.

3. Display the drop down list of **Flag to** reasons, but leave the option as **Follow up**.

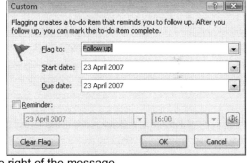

4. Leave the **Start date** as today's date but change the **Due date** to a future date then click **OK**. A coloured flag appears at the right of the message.

> *To display all flagged messages together, click in the header of the flag column in the **Inbox**.*

5. Use the techniques described earlier to add the following headings to the **Inbox**; **Start Date**, **Due Date**, **Flag Completed Date**.

Size	Start Date	Due Date	Flag Complete...	🏳
11 KB	Mon 23/04/2007	Tue 24/04/2007	None	🏳

6. Click the **Flag** icon for the message to mark it as complete. The flag changes to a tick and the **Flag Completed Date** is added.

7. Flag another message.

8. To remove a flag either, click the **Follow Up** button and select **Clear Flag** or right click on an actual flag and select **Clear Flag**. Remove the **Flag** just set by using either method.

9. Select **View | Current View | Customize Current View | Reset Current View** to return the **Inbox** headings to their default settings. Click **OK** and **OK** again.

Driving Lesson 18 - Attaching Files

▣ Park and Read

It is possible to attach any sort of file to an e-mail message in *Outlook,* provided it doesn't exceed the size the destination mailbox will allow (if this is the case the message will be returned undelivered). This makes it easy to send reports, charts, sound files or pictures, for example. When the message reaches its destination, the paperclip icon adjacent to the envelope, 🖂 📎 , will let the recipient know there is an attachment.

⬈ Manoeuvres

1. Within **Inbox**, click on the **New Mail Message** button, 📧 New ▾ .

2. Enter a friend's e-mail address (or your own) in the **To** box and enter the **Subject** as **Attachment**.

3. In the message area, type the following text:

    Could you look at the attached file and let me know which wines you want to order for the party next week?

4. Click the **Attach File** button, 📎 Attach File and the **Insert File** dialog box will appear.

5. Select the location where the ECDL word processing data files are stored (a folder named **3 Word Processing**), then double click on the **Winelist** file to attach it.

6. If the message is being created in HTML format (the default), all attachments appear on a new **Attached:** line under the **Subject**.

Subject:	Attachment
Attached:	📄 Winelist.docx (12 KB)

ℹ️ *If the message is being created in **Rich Text** format, attachments will appear as icons in the text area of the message.*

7. To attach a second file, repeat steps **4** and **5**, this time double clicking the **Banking** file from the same location.

8. The **Banking** file has been attached in error. To delete this attachment, select its entry in the **Attached** box, then press <**Delete**>.

9. Click ✉ Send , then 📩 Send/Receive to send the message together with its attachment.

10. Leave *Outlook* open.

Driving Lesson 19 - Open and Save a File Attachment

🅿 Park and Read

When a message with an attachment is received, it can be opened, saved, or both. You should be aware that some anti-virus protection and firewall software can prevent you receiving certain types of attachment. If you are connected to a network – in an office for example – it may also have been set up to prevent access to these types of attachment. Typically, problems may occur when receiving files with an **.exe** or **.mdb** extension. These files run scripts and macros in order to function – so do many types of virus. Attachments are a common way for viruses to be introduced to your system. Be very wary of opening any attachment if you are not absolutely sure of its source.

Manoeuvres

1. Within **Inbox**, create a new message and enter your own e-mail address in the **To** box. Enter the subject as **Saving Attachments**.

2. In the message area, type **The attached file may be of interest to you.**

3. Attach the **Maneaters** file from the ECDL word processing data files, as described in the previous Driving Lesson.

4. Click ⌐ **Send**, then 📧 **Send/Receive** to send the message.

5. If necessary, wait a few seconds before clicking 📧 **Send/Receive** again. The message is displayed in the **Inbox** with an attachment icon.

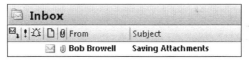

ℹ️ *It is possible that Outlook will identify this message as **Junk Mail** and store it in a special **Junk E-mail** folder. If so, open the **Junk E-mail** folder from the **Folders Pane**, select the **Saving Attachments** message and click the **Not Junk** button,* *. The message will be moved to the **Inbox**.*

6. Double click on the message to open it.

7. To open the attachment, right click on the **Maneaters** icon in the message and select **Open** from the shortcut menu (or double click the icon). Attachments are a common source of computer viruses so a security message may be displayed. If so, click **Open**.

☞

Driving Lesson 19 - Continued

8. *Word* starts, displaying the contents of the attached file. Read the file then close *Word*.

9. To save the attachment without opening it (so that it could be checked for viruses for example), right click on the **Maneaters** icon in the message and select **Save As** from the shortcut menu.

10. When the **Save Attachment** dialog box is displayed, ensure that the save location is **Documents**.

> **i**   If **Documents** is not shown by default, select it from **Favorite Links** or locate it in the **Folders** list on the left of the dialog box.

11. Click **Save** to save the attached file or files.

12. Open the **Documents** folder from the **Start** menu to see the file then close the **Documents** window and close the message window.

13. Attachments can be saved without opening the message. Make sure the **Saving Attachments** message is selected within **Inbox**.

14. Select **File | Save Attachments**, then **Maneaters.doc**.

15. The **Save Attachment** dialog box is displayed again. As there already is a saved copy of this file, click **Cancel** to close the dialog box.

> **i**   Outlook will not open certain file types (such as **.exe** or **.bat** files) that are more likely to contain viruses. Depending on the security settings they will be handled in one of two ways;
> a) the files will be totally inaccessible and a note will appear at the top of the message listing all such attached files.
> b) the files will be shown but can only be saved so they can be virus checked.

Driving Lesson 20 - Changing Message Priority

🅿 Park and Read

Messages have **Normal** priority by default, but it is possible to change their priority to either **High** or **Low**. This does not mean that they are sent more quickly or slowly, only that the recipient will be aware of their urgency by an icon at the left of the message.

Manoeuvres

1.   Start a new message.

2.   Address it to yourself and enter the subject as **Urgent!**

3.   In the message area, type **Don't forget the meeting with the area manager at 2pm today.**

4.   Make sure the **Message** tab is displayed on the **Ribbon** and click the **High Importance** button, `High Importance`

5.   Send the message, then after a few seconds, click `Send/Receive`.

6.   When the message arrives in the **Inbox**, it will have an **Importance** icon set.

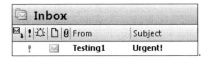

7.   Open the message. A bar appears across the top of the message to show that it is high priority.

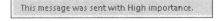

ℹ️ *The process to make a message low priority is the same. Select the **Low Importance** button from the Ribbon. It will have a low importance icon when it is received. When opened, the bar on the message will indicate that it is Low Importance.*

8.   Close the message.

Driving Lesson 21 - Reply to/Forward Messages

▣ Park and Read

A user can reply to the sender of a message, or reply to all the recipients of a message as well as the original sender. A message form will appear where the reply can be entered (the original message will be underneath for reference). A message can also be forwarded to someone who wasn't on the original send list.

☞ Manoeuvres

1. Within **Inbox**, select the message named **Urgent**.

2. Click on the **Reply** button, [Reply], to display a message form, addressed to the sender of the original message. The original message is displayed.

ⓘ *The **Reply to All** button,* [Reply to All] *, is used to send the reply to all recipients of the original message.*

3. If you never want the original message to appear in the replies you send, it can be omitted automatically. Minimise the reply message form to activate the main menus and select **Tools | Options** and the **Preferences** tab.

4. Click **E-mail Options** and open the drop down list from **When replying to a message**.

5. Select **Do not include original message**.

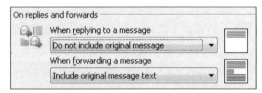

6. Clock **OK** then **OK** again.

7. Maximise the **Urgent** message and close it <u>without</u> saving.

8. To see the effect of the new settings, click again. Notice how the original message is not included.

9. The **Subject** section begins with **Re:** indicating a reply to a previous message. After **Re:**, delete the existing subject and replace it with **Replying to messages**.

Driving Lesson 21 - Continued

10. Enter the following message text:

    I was aware of the meeting. There is no need for concern, but thank you for your message.

11. Click **Send**, then **Send and Receive**.

12. To change the settings to their usual status, select **Tools | Options** and the **Preferences** tab, click **E-mail Options** and select **Include original message text** for the **replying** option.

13. Click **OK** to confirm the change, then **OK** again.

14. Select the **Urgent** message and click the **Reply** button. The original message is shown but can be deleted manually - use the mouse to highlight the text, then delete it. (This method is used to remove an original message from the current reply only).

15. Close the message window <u>without</u> saving.

16. Select the **Urgent** message again, then click the **Forward** button, Forward . When the message form is displayed, click in **To** and enter a friend's address.

17. The **Subject** section begins with **FW:** indicating a forward message. The forwarding message can be typed in the main window, leaving the original message underneath for reference. In the **Subject** box, enter **Forwarding messages**.

18. In the message area, enter the following text, above the original message:

    This message is forwarded as part of Module 7 of the ECDL.

19. Click **Send**. The message has been forwarded to a friend.

20. Leave *Outlook* open.

Driving Lesson 22 - Contacts

▣ Park and Read

To avoid typing addresses onto every e-mail message, lists of known addresses can be stored by *Outlook* in the Address Book. If *Outlook* is being used on a network a **Global Address List** will be available, listing the details and e-mail addresses of all users on the network. This is maintained by the network administrator. It is also possible for any user to create a personal list (stored within the **Contacts** folder in *Outlook*), which lists the details of specific, personal contacts.

↳ Manoeuvres

1. Select **Tools | Address Book** to display the **Address Book**.

2. The **Global Address List** may be displayed by default. It is not possible to add names to this list unless you are an administrator. Click on the drop down arrow under **Address Book** and select **Contacts**.

ℹ *There may be no **Contacts** records present if none have been added yet.*

3. From the **Address Book** window select **File | New Entry**. Select **New Contact** and click **OK**.

4. Enter your own details in the relevant boxes. There are many possible fields but only **Full Name** and **E-mail** address are required for this guide. Click **Save & Close** to add the entry.

ℹ *Details in the **Contacts** list can also be maintained and created from the* ***Contacts** folder of Outlook.*

5. In the same way, add the names and details of four friends to the address book.

ℹ *Someone in the **Global Address List** can be added to the **Contacts** list by right clicking their name and selecting **Add to Contacts**.*

6. Close the **Address Book**.

Driving Lesson 23 - Add Sender to Contacts

▣ Park and Read

When a message is received from a contact, there is a quick and easy way to add that contact's details to your address book.

↰ Manoeuvres

1. Open any message from your **Inbox** and right click on the **From** address.

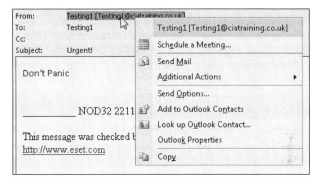

2. Select **Add to Outlook Contacts** from the shortcut menu. When the contact form appears, add any further details that may be required, then click **Save & Close**.

3. Close the message.

4. Open the **Address Book**, select **Contacts** and make sure you can see the new entry.

5. Close the **Address Book**.

6. The contact that was just added to the address book has decided to move to a deserted island, without leaving a forwarding address. Open the **Address Book** again and display **Contacts**.

7. Select the new contact and press the <**Delete**> key. Click **Yes** at the prompt to delete the contact's details.

8. Close the **Address Book**, but leave the **Inbox** open.

Driving Lesson 24 - Distribution Lists

▣ Park and Read

It is possible to create **Distribution Lists** of specific contacts, so that messages can be sent to groups of people with a single click of the mouse. Multiple distribution lists can be created, each containing particular types of contact, such as family, darts team, friends, etc. Any contact can belong to more than one list.

☞ Manoeuvres

1. To create a distribution list from an existing address book, open the **Address Book**. Select **File | New Entry** and select **New Distribution List**.

2. Click **OK** to display the **Untitled - Distribution List** window.

3. Enter **Friends** in the **Name** box. This is the name of the distribution list.

4. Click **Select Members** from the **Ribbon**. Make sure **Contacts** is selected in the top drop down box, then double click on a name from the list, to add them to the list of **Members** shown at the bottom of the dialog box.

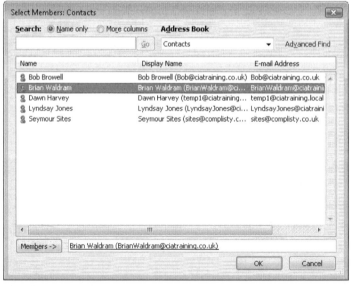

5. Repeat the process to add two other friends to the list. Multiple selections can be made using any technique then several records can be added at once.

Driving Lesson 24 - Continued

6.   Click **OK** to return to the **Friends Distribution List** window..

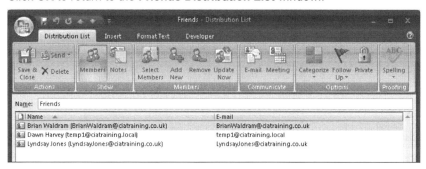

*Notice there are buttons here to **Select** more members for the list, **Add New** members who are not currently in the Address Book, and **Remove** members from the list. Removing members does not delete them from the Address Book.*

7.   Click **Save & Close**. The **Friends** distribution group is added to the **Contacts Address Book**. Display the **Contacts** list to see it.

🧑 Dawn Harvey	Dawn Harvey (temp1@ciatraining..
👥 Friends	**Friends**
🧑 Lyndsay Jones	Lyndsay Jones (LyndsayJones@ci.

8.   Close the **Address Book** and compose a new message. To send the message to everyone on the **Friends** contact group, click on ⬚To... . Display **Contacts**. The **Friends** group appears with the other contacts.

9.   Double click on **Friends** from the list to add it as the target address, then click **OK**. The group name is added to the message.

10. The message will be sent to all addresses included in the **Friends** distribution list. Enter the subject as **Contact Groups**.

11. Type in a suitable message and send it.

*Once the message is sent, all the individual addresses in the distribution list will be shown the **To** address box.*

*To send the same message to several people in the Contacts who are not on a distribution list, click ⬚To... , then double click on each required name, before clicking **OK**.*

Driving Lesson 25 - Revision

This covers the features introduced in this section. Try not to refer to the preceding Driving Lessons while completing it.

1. Check for any new messages in the **Inbox**.

2. Read any that may have arrived.

3. Select any single message that has been read and mark it as unread.

4. Flag the selected message.

5. Remove the flag.

6. Close any open messages.

7. Open the **Contacts Address Book** and add three new entries, using the names and addresses of colleagues.

8. Create a new distribution list in **Contacts**, named **Colleagues** and add the new entries to it.

9. Create a new message and address it to the **Colleagues** distribution list and enter the subject as **Diet**.

10. Attach the file **Calories** (located in the **ECDL** subfolder **4 Spreadsheets**).

11. Enter the message text as follows:

    I thought this calorie counter might be useful for those of us starting the new wonder diet.

12. Make the message **High Priority** and then send it.

If you experienced any difficulty completing the Revision, refer back to the Driving Lessons in this section. Then redo the Revision.

Driving Lesson 26 - Revision

This covers the features introduced in this section. Try not to refer to the preceding Driving Lessons while completing it.

1.   Start a new message and address it to yourself.

2.   Send a copy to a friend or colleague.

3.   Enter the **Subject** as **Web Page**.

4.   Attach the file **Images.htm** that was saved in the **Documents** folder as part of the Internet guide, Driving Lesson 33. If you do not have this file choose any other.

5.   Enter the body of the message as **Have a look at the web site in the attached file**.

6.   Send the message.

7.   After a minute check for incoming mail.

8.   When the **Web Page** message arrives save the attachment in **Documents**.

9.   Overwrite the original file if prompted, as the attachment is exactly the same.

If you experienced any difficulty completing the Revision, refer back to the Driving Lessons in this section. Then redo the Revision.

Driving Lesson 27 - Revision

This covers the features introduced in this section. Try not to refer to the preceding Driving Lessons while completing it.

1.   Create a distribution list named **Staff**.

2.   Add three friends or colleagues to the list.

3.   Create a new message.

4.   Address the message to the **Staff** distribution list.

5.   Send a carbon copy to yourself.

6.   Enter the **Subject** as **Team Building Trip**.

7.   Make the message high priority.

8.   Enter the following message:

> **This month's outing is to a local paint balling range. Please let me know if you are free on Friday week.**

9.   Send the message.

10.   Check for incoming mail.

11.   Flag the **Team Building Trip** message.

12.   Reply to the message, saying that you are free.

13.   Send the message.

If you experienced any difficulty completing the Revision, refer back to the Driving Lessons in this section. Then redo the Revision.

Once you are confident with the features, complete the Record of Achievement Matrix referring to the section at the end of the guide. Only when competent move on to the next Section.

Section 4
Message
Management

By the end of this Section you should be able to:

Save a Draft Message

Print Messages

Delete Messages

Organise Messages in Folders

To gain an understanding of the above features, work through the **Driving Lessons** in this **Section**.

For each **Driving Lesson**, read the **Park and Read** instructions, without touching the keyboard, then work through the numbered steps of the **Manoeuvres** on the computer. Complete the **Revision Exercise(s)** at the end of the section to test your knowledge.

Driving Lesson 28 - Save a Draft Message

⊞ Park and Read

Occasionally, you may be in the middle of typing a message when you have to leave it, perhaps to check information. This doesn't mean the message is lost - you can save a draft copy and come back to it later.

↱ Manoeuvres

1.   Within **Inbox**, start a new message with the subject **Meeting**.

2.   Type in the message **Are you available for the staffing meeting on**.

3.   You need to check the date of the meeting. Click the **Close** button on the message. The following prompt appears:

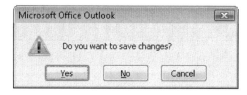

4.   Click **Yes**. The information message shows it's been saved.

i   *Alternatively to save to **Drafts** click the **Office Button** and then select **Save** or press <**Ctrl S**> and then **Close** the message.*

5.   Click **OK** if a confirmation message is displayed.

6.   Notice the **Drafts** icon, ⌄ Drafts [1] , in the **Folder List**, showing there is a single draft message.

i   *To continue a draft message at a later stage, click the **Drafts** folder. Double click on the message to open it and continue as usual.*

Driving Lesson 29 - Printing a Message

▣ Park and Read

Messages can be printed by simply opening the desired message, then selecting the print command. The number of copies and print range can be selected as required.

↱ Manoeuvres

1. Within **Inbox**, select any message but do not open it.

2. Select **File | Print** or press **<Ctrl P>**. The **Print** dialog box is displayed.

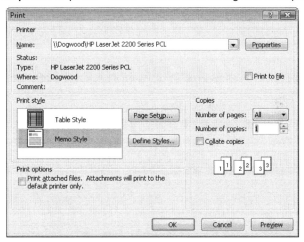

3. The dialog box has a **Preview** button to view the message before printing if required. Click **Preview** to print preview the message. Click **Print** to return to the **Print** dialog box (clicking **Close**, closes the **Preview** window and returns to the **Inbox**.

ℹ *Messages can be previewed directly from the Inbox by selecting File | Print Preview.*

4. In **Number of copies**, use the up spinner to increase the number to **2**. Click **OK** to print two copies of the e-mail.

5. Select a different message from the **Inbox** (do not open it by double clicking). Click the **Print** button, 🖨, on the **Standard Toolbar** to print one copy of the entire e-mail to the default printer.

ℹ *If a message is open, click the Office Button, 🔘, and then select Print.*

6. Close the message, but leave the **Inbox** open.

Driving Lesson 30 - Deleting Messages

■ Park and Read

All messages received are stored in the **Inbox**. After a period of time these messages will need to be deleted. Once selected, messages can be deleted and are moved from the **Inbox** to the **Deleted Items** folder, a temporary store, until confirmation of permanent deletion.

Manoeuvres

1. In the **Inbox**, select the **Test message**.

i *To select all messages, press <Ctrl A>; to select non adjacent messages hold the <Ctrl> key and click the required messages; to select a range, use the <Shift> key.*

2. Click the **Delete** button, ⊠, on the toolbar and the message is deleted.

3. Scroll down the **Folders List** and select Deleted Items. The information viewer will now show all deleted messages.

4. To retrieve the **Test message** and replace it in the **Inbox**, right click on it, then select **Move to Folder**. From the list in the **Move Items** dialog box, locate and select **Inbox**, then click **OK**.

i *A deleted message can also be clicked and dragged from where it is being viewed in the Deleted Items folder, to the required folder on the Folders List.*

5. View the **Inbox** folder to see that the message has been retrieved.

6. Delete the message again, but this time use the <**Delete**> key, which is an alternative method.

7. View the **Deleted Items** folder; the message has reappeared.

8. To empty the **Deleted Items** folder, right click Deleted Items and select **Empty 'Deleted Items' Folder** from the menu.

9. In the **Warning message** box, select **Yes** and the messages will be permanently deleted.

Driving Lesson 31 - Creating Inbox Folders

▣ Park and Read

If the same computer is being used by several people, it may be a good idea to create a system of folders in which to store their individual messages. Once folders have been set up, messages can be sent directly to them on receipt. Messages can be moved between folders as required. Unwanted folders can be deleted.

⌐ Manoeuvres

1. To create your own mail folder within the **Inbox**, first make sure the **Inbox** is selected in the **Folders List** and then select **File | New | Folder**.

2. In the **Folder name** box, type in your first name and click **OK**. The new folder has been created.

3. The display in the **Folders List** changes to show the location of the new folder. If the structure within **Inbox** is ever hidden, expand it by clicking the icon to the left, 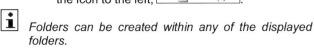.

ℹ️ *Folders can be created within any of the displayed folders.*

ℹ️ *To delete a folder, right click on it and select* **Delete**.

Driving Lesson 31 - Continued

4.   To arrange for your incoming mail to be sent to the new folder, select **Tools | Rules and Alerts** then click the **New Rule** button in the **Rules and Alerts** dialog box. The **Rules Wizard** dialog box will be displayed.

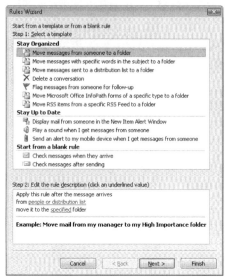

5.   The first screen is to select a template if required. In this Lesson the rule will be set up manually so click **Next** to select the **Conditions** for the rule.

6.   Uncheck the existing **Condition** selections then check **where my name is in the To box**. Click **Next** to select the rule **Actions**.

7.   Make sure the action **move it to the specified folder** is selected from the list of actions. The rule description should now look like this:

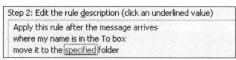

8.   Now click the word **specified** to select the folder to which incoming mail can be forwarded. Locate and select your folder then click **OK**.

9.   Click **Finish** to complete the process then click **OK** to close the dialog box.

10.   All mail addressed to you will now be placed in the new folder, not the Inbox. Test the rule by sending yourself a message.

11.   Select **Tools | Rules and Alerts** to display the **Rules and Alerts** dialog box, select the rule just created and click **Delete**. Click **Yes** to confirm then click **OK** to close the dialog box.

Driving Lesson 32 - Organising Messages

▣ Park and Read

Once folders have been created, messages can be moved between them if necessary. It is also possible to sort messages in various ways.

↱ Manoeuvres

1. Make sure the **Inbox** is the folder being viewed.

2. To sort the messages by name of sender, click on the **From** heading at the top of the message pane.

3. To sort the messages by date and time received, click on the **Received** heading. The default order is to show the most recent first. This is useful as new messages will always appear at the top. Click the heading again to sort them in the reverse date order, then click again to restore the default order.

i *Messages can be sorted in the same way by any column header, e.g. **Priority, Attachment, Size** or **Subject**.*

4. Select any message from the **Inbox**. To move it to your folder, first make sure that your folder is visible in the **Folders List**. Right click on the message and select **Move to Folder** from the shortcut menu.

5. Select your folder from the list in the **Move** dialog box and click **OK**. The message has been moved. Open your folder to check.

i *Messages can be moved to any folder on the **Folders List** by clicking and dragging.*

6. In the **Inbox**, sort all the messages by date received, with the most recently received messages at the top.

7. Select your folder in the **Folders List** and press <**Delete**>. A confirmation box is displayed.

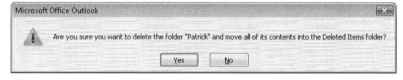

8. Click **Yes** then expand the **Deleted Items** folder to show your folder.

9. Select your folder from within **Deleted Items** and press <**Delete**>. Another box is displayed to confirm the permanent deletion of the folder. Select **Yes** and the folder is removed from the computer.

Driving Lesson 33 - Finding Messages

▣ Park and Read

It is also possible to search for messages in various ways. For example, messages from a particular person, with a specific subject or content.

☞ Manoeuvres

1. To search for particular message content, view the **Inbox** and locate the **Search** box at the right of the **Inbox** window.

2. Type **attachment** in the **Search** box, [attachment _____ |x|▼].

3. As the word is being entered the **Inbox** will be searched for entries which contain the text.

ⓘ *The default search option is to search <u>all</u> of the text in the messages for a match so the above example would find any messages where the search word appeared in the **Subject**, the **Body** of the message or the **To** and **From** fields.*

4. Click the cross, ⌧, in the **Search** box to clear it and display all messages again.

5. For more complex searches, click the chevrons, ⌄⌄, to the right of the **Search** box to expand the **Query Builder**.

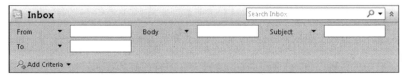

6. Now search criteria can be entered for specific areas of the message. In the **Subject** box, type **Sending**. Any message with **sending** in the **Subject** field will be selected. Messages with **sending** only in the body of the message will not be selected.

ⓘ *If a consistent system of labelling **Subjects** on messages is used, it will be possible to search for all messages relating to a particular subject.*

7. Click the cross, ⌧, in the **Search** box to clear all search criteria.

Driving Lesson 33 - Continued

8. The areas in the expanded search can be changed. Click the drop down arrow to the right of **Body** and select **Importance** from the drop down list.

9. Click in the new search box for **Importance**. The three possible options are listed. Click on **High** to find any messages flagged as high importance.

10. Change the Importance field back to **Body** and click the chevrons, 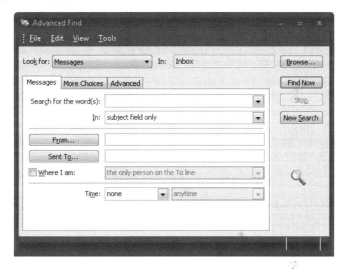, to close the **Query Builder**.

11. Select **Tools | Instant Search** to see a list of searching features, including **Instant Search** and **Query Builder** which have already been described.

12. Select **Advanced Find**.

13. This function allows complex searches to be made across all *Outlook* areas such as **Messages**, **Contacts** and **Tasks**. Enter **manager** in the **Search for the words(s):** box and select **subject field and message body** from the **In:** box.

14. Click **Find Now**. Notice the message(s) displayed at the bottom of the box.

15. Double click on the message to open it. Check for the text **area manager**.

16. Examine all the other options available then close the **Advanced Find** window.

Driving Lesson 34 - Revision

This covers the features introduced in this section. Try not to refer to the preceding Driving Lessons while completing it.

1.   Open the **Team Building Trip** message.

2.   Print three copies.

3.   Print the first sentence of the message text only.

4.   Close the message.

5.   Organise all messages in your **Inbox** by **Subject** in ascending alphabetical order.

6.   Print the first message in the list.

7.   Search for any messages in the **Inbox** with the message text containing the word **team**.

8.   Search for any messages with attachments.

9.   Search for any messages that have been flagged.

10. Close the **Find Message** dialog box.

11. Create a new folder in the **Inbox**, called **ECDL Module 7**.

12. Move all of the messages created during this module into the new folder.

13. Sort the messages by date received, with the most recent at the top of the list.

14. Search for any messages received from yourself.

15. Print these messages, then delete them.

16. Empty the **Deleted Items** folder.

17. Close *Outlook*.

If you experienced any difficulty completing the Revision, refer back to the Driving Lessons in this section. Then redo the Revision.

Once you are confident with the features, complete the Record of Achievement Matrix referring to the section at the end of the guide.

Answers

Driving Lesson 7

Step 1   E-mail is beneficial for businesses because it is very fast, cheap and web based accounts can be accessed from any computer with Internet access.

Step 2   **Netiquette** is network etiquette: a set of rules governing how you should use e-mail.

Step 3   Messages may contain viruses.

Step 4   Make sure you have up to date anti-virus software installed. Save attachments and scan them before opening if you are suspicious.

Step 5   E-mail is electronic mail.

Step 6   An e-mail address consists of a **user name**, an **@ sign** and a **domain name**.

Glossary

Address Bar	Shows the address of the page currently displayed in the Browser and allows entry of a new address to be visited.
Attachment	Any file transmitted with an e-mail.
Distribution List	A grouping of several mail addresses than can be accessed with a single name.
Folder	A method of grouping together files (and other folders).
Forward (a message)	Send a copy of an e-mail which you have received, to another address, with an optional message of your own.
Inbox	The default folder for storing all incoming e-mail messages.
Mail Rules	Definable rules on how to treat incoming e-mails depending on certain conditions.
Outbox	The folder for storing outgoing e-mails before they have been sent.
Preview Pane	An area of the **Inbox** display screen where the contents of messages can be viewed without opening them.
Recycle Bin	An area of storage where deleted files are held temporarily before being deleted completely.
Sent Items	The folder for storing outgoing e-mails after they have been sent.
Subfolder	A folder that is contained within another folder.

Index

Address Book 40

    Add Sender to 41

Applying a Signature 26

Attaching Files 34

    Open 35

    Save 35

Closing

    Outlook 17

Copying

    From Word 23

    Messages 22

Creating

    Inbox Folders 51

    Message 20

Cut

    Messages 22

    Text from Word 23

Contacts 40

    Add Sender to 41

Deleting Messages 50

Distribution Lists 42

E-mail

    Changing Screen Display 13

    Closing Outlook 17

    Help 12

    Online Help Functions 12

    Outlook 10

    Using 8

Finding

    Messages 54

Flag a Message 33

Forwarding Messages 38

Help

    E-mail 12

Identity Theft 9

Inbox Folders 51

Messages

    Change Priority 37

    Copy 22

    Create 20

    Cut 22

    Delete 50

    Find 54

    Flag 33

    Forward 38

    Headings 15

    Open 32

    Organising 53

    Paste 22, 23

    Print 49

    Priority 37

    Read 32

    Reply to 38

    Send 31

Netiquette 8

Open Messages 32

Organising

    Messages 53

Outlook

    Closing 17

    Opening 10

Paste

    from Word 23

    Messages 22

Phishing 9

Printing

    E-mail Message 49

Read Messages 32

Replying to Messages 38

Revision

Message Editing 28-29

Message Management 56

Outlook 18

Send and Receive 44-46

Saving

Attachments 35

Draft Messages 48

Security

E-mail 9

Sending Messages 31

Signature

Applying 26

Spell Checker 24

Views

Changing Display 13

Record of Achievement Matrix

This Matrix is to be used to measure your progress while working through the guide. This is a learning reinforcement process, you judge when you are competent.

Tick boxes are provided for each feature. 1 is for no knowledge, 2 some knowledge and 3 is for competent. A section is only complete when column 3 is completed for all parts of the section.

For details on sitting ECDL Examinations in your country please contact the local ECDL Licensee or visit the European Computer Driving Licence Foundation Limited web site at http://www.ecdl.com.

Tick the Relevant Boxes **1**: No Knowledge   **2**: Some Knowledge   **3**: Competent

Section	No	Driving Lesson	1	2	3
1 Outlook	1	Using E-mail			
	2	Using Outlook			
	3	E-mail Help			
	4	Changing Screen Display			
	5	Message Headings			
	6	Closing Outlook			
2 Message Editing	8	Creating a Message			
	9	Cut, Copy and Paste Messages			
	10	Cut, Copy and Paste from Word			
	11	Spell Checker			
	12	Applying a Signature			
3 Send and Receive	15	Sending Messages			
	16	Open and Read Messages			
	17	Flagging a Message			
	18	Attaching Files			
	19	Open and Save a File Attachment			
	20	Changing Message Priority			
	21	Reply to / Forward Messages			
	22	Contacts			
	23	Add Sender to Contacts			
	24	Distribution Lists			
4 Message Management	28	Save a Draft Message			
	29	Printing a Message			
	30	Deleting Messages			
	31	Creating Inbox Folders			
	32	Organising Messages			
	33	Finding Messages			

Other Products from CiA Training

CiA Training is a leading publishing company, which has consistently delivered the highest quality products since 1985. A wide range of flexible and easy to use self teach resources has been developed by CiA's experienced publishing team to aid the learning process. These include the following materials at the time of publication of this product:

- **ECDL/ICDL Syllabus 5.0 (ECDL Foundation Qualification)**
  - Module 1 - Concepts of Information Technology (IT)
  - Module 2 - Using the Computer and Managing Files
  - Module 3 - Word Processing
  - Module 4 - Spreadsheets
  - Module 5 - Database
  - Module 6 - Presentation
  - Module 7 - Information and Communication

- **ECDL/ICDL Advanced (ECDL Foundation Qualification)**
  - Advanced Module AM3 Word Processing
  - Advanced Module AM4 Spreadsheets
  - Advanced Module AM5 Database
  - Advanced Module AM6 Presentation

- **Revision Books (Support Materials for ECDL/ICDL Qualifications)**
  - Core Syllabus (All 7 modules in a single book)
  - Advanced AM3 Word Processing
  - Advanced AM4 Spreadsheets
  - Advanced AM5 Database
  - Advanced AM6 Presentation

- **e-Citizen Book (ECDL Foundation Qualification)**

We hope you have enjoyed using our materials and would love to hear your opinions about them. If you'd like to give us some feedback, please go to:

www.ciatraining.co.uk/feedback.php

and let us know what you think.

New products are constantly being developed. For up to the minute information on our products, to view our full range, to find out more, or to be added to our mailing list, visit:

www.ciatraining.co.uk

Notes